T0128544

THE MASTER'S WELL DONE!

———— ✣ ————

DR. JOHN THOMAS WYLIE

authorHOUSE®

AuthorHouse™
1663 Liberty Drive
Bloomington, IN 47403
www.authorhouse.com
Phone: 1 (800) 839-8640

Published by AuthorHouse 05/22/2020

ISBN: 978-1-7283-6262-5 (sc)
ISBN: 978-1-7283-6261-8 (e)

Contents

CHAPTER TWO

CHAPTER THREE

A Special Dedication

I AM PROUD TO dedicate this publication, "The Master's Well-Done," to Jaqui McCree, who presently resides in Radcliff, Kentucky; and is the proud son of Jo Ann and Jackie McCree. Shortly after Jaqui completed high school, he enlisted in the US Marine Corps for four years. Upon completing his tour of duty in the US Marine Corps, Jaqui enlisted in the US Army for an additional four years. He was awarded an honorable discharge for his military service to his country.

After completing military service he began work as a civilian contractor as a Human Resources Specialist in South Korea and Japan (2008-2018). Jaqui is happily married to a loving, faithful Christian wife, Frehiwot, from Addis Ababa, Ethiopia and have two children of whom they cherish.

He is a Christian gentleman and possesses a burning desire to lead souls to Jesus Christ. He stated of himself, "I am a representative of Jesus Christ and intend to seek the lost for Him with the hope of conveying the message of salvation to the lost." Jaqui also has organized a group Bible study, a prayer group at his work and home, and is preparing Christian pamphlets to encourage the lost to Christ.

I am proud of this young Christian man who seeks to do the will of the Lord without any reservations. I encourage him that: "The Will of God' will never lead you where "The Grace of God" cannot keep you." Continue your efforts in the great service and work of the Lord Jesus Christ until you one day hear him say: "My Good and faithful Servant, Well-Done!"

Jaqui is a young Christian who is willing to help others, witnessing, praying, giving time and energy to God's work; as well as being a living testimony to the world he lives in. He knows how to be still and wait on the Lord. The Christian life has its difficulties, but victory is assured because: "Greater is He who is in you, than he who is in the world" (I John 4:4 NASB). Jesus said, "Follow me, and I will make you fishers of men" (Matthew 4:19 KJV).

The Apostle Paul wrote: "I have fought the good fight, I have finished the course, I have kept the faith: henceforth there is laid up for me the crown of righteousness, which the Lord, the righteous judge, shall give to me as that day; and not to me only, but also to all them that have loved his appearing" (II Timothy 4:7, 8 KJV).

Prayerfully In Christ,
Your Faithful, Loving Uncle,
Reverend Dr. John Thomas Wylie

Introduction

THIS PUBLICATION, "THE MASTER'S Well-Done," is a book on The Stewardship of Prayer, Evangelism (Soul-winning), and The Master's Well-Done.

The First Phase of our publication is concerned about the Stewardship of Prayer. Many churches in the land, just as a considerable lot of its individuals from those churches, have neglected to profit themselves of the spiritual power that may be theirs if they followed the claim of early Christians and tarried in the upper room until they, as well, were endued with power from on high.

Many Christians experience life with their spirits incredibly undernourished spiritually, and that amidst God's boundless abundance from which we are allowed to choose those nourishments that are expected to make us strong, happy, and useful in the service of the Lord. "Ye have not because ye ask not." (James 4:2 KJV).

The second phase of this publication concerns Soul-Winning (Evangelism). What number of individuals from your church truly put forth any genuine attempt to win others (souls) to Christ?

Since there are in a portion of our churches a few laborers who win various others to Christ during the year, and a significant number of the callings are because of the works of Pastor, evangelists, preachers, the genuine number of soul-winners is far less than what we would anticipate.

Each Christian who has ever occupied themselves with it will affirm that triumphant spirits carries larger fulfillments to the laborer than some other phase of service on earth. The

Bible likewise reveals that the rewards for soul-winning on the earth to come will be bigger than those for some other phase of Christian effort in which we can engage.

Jesus Christ said, "The field is the world" (Matthew 13:38 KJV). Jesus also said, "Go ye therefore, and make disciples of all the nations" (Matthew 28:19 KJV).

At long last the third phase of this publication concerns the Master's Well-Done. The Bible gives us reason to believe that there will be degrees of reward in heaven depending on our faithfulness in this life. We can't theorize on the character of these rewards, however we can expect that God has revealed this truth as a stimulus to loyalty, faithfulness and effort. It is beyond imagination or not possible to suppose that the church member who neglects spiritual responsibilities will have the status in heaven as the good steward who gives himself and his means unsparingly for the cause of Jesus Christ. For the latter, heaven will begin with his Master's approving "Well-Done."

The commendation and reward for faithful service have already been provided and laid aside in heaven awaiting the arrival of the steward in the presence of his Lord, according to Paul, who wrote:

"I have fought the good fight, I have finished the course, I have kept the faith: henceforth there is laid up for me the crown of righteousness, which the Lord, the righteous judge, shall give to me at that day; and not to me only, but also to all them that have love his appearing (II Timothy 4:7,8 KJV).

However, the reward of the faithful Christian is not all deferred to the future. Loyalty to Jesus Christ and his church brings present felicities as well as lasting joys to come. The truly happy Christian is the committed Christian whose happiness is in the joy of service, and for whom heaven awaits.

(All scripture references are of the AV version, the KJV unless otherwise indicated).

Chapter
ONE

The Stewardship Of Prayer

Why Be Hungry In The
Midst Of Plenty?

MIGHT YOU BE ABLE to envision a seriously eager man walking past a huge table, intensely loaded up with a wide range of tempting food, free for the taking, and not taking such food as would fulfill his craving? Such folly would mark him as intellectually unsound (mentally unsound). Be that as it may, we see a tremendous number of all professing Christians experiencing life with their souls incredibly undernourished, and that amidst God's boundless abundance from which we are allowed to choose only those nourishments that are expected to make us strong, cheerful, and useful.

"Ye Have Not, Because Ye Ask Not"
(James 4:2 KJV)

AS WAS THE CASE in the day of John the Baptist, so it is likewise today, "A man can get nothing, aside from it have been given him from heaven" (John 3:27). We were unable to live an hour without using the resources which a generous Heavenly Father places available to us without asking, or as often as possible without our awareness regarding their source.

However, these gifts which we appreciate without looking for are extremely little undoubtedly contrasted with the bigger advantages and fulfillments that would be our own if we just went to God and requested them. As James reminded us in his epistle, "Ye have not, because ye ask not" (James 4:2 KJV).

God Stands Ready To Supply Our Needs (Philippians 4:19 KJV)

THEN AGAIN WE ARE guaranteed by Paul that, "My God shall supply every need of yours as per his riches in glory in Christ Jesus" (Phil. 4:19 ASV). It is safe to say that we are not without excuse, at that point, when we proceed just to exist in the Christian life, lacking grace and strength with which to achieve that growth in personal character and that usefulness in God's service that would be acceptable to him who made us, who provided our redemption through his begotten Son, and who surrounds every single one of us from day to day with all the uncounted blessings that are our own?

Churches Should Put "New Emphasis" on "Prayer"

CHRISTIANS ALL THROUGH THE globe number millions upon millions, from different denominations, with countless church associations, their capable pastors, missionaries, evangelists, preachers and other church pioneers, their universal conventions, and the sanctification of their tremendous riches, could without much of a stretch become the best Christians the world has ever known.

In any case, it is vital that they get a vision of their potential outcomes in prayer and afterward accomplish those conceivable outcomes by truly captivating in that kind of supplication which God's Word teaches us is acceptable to the Father.

Maybe we have to reevaluate the character of the Wednesday night services as held in most of our churches. By custom, these have been known as prayer meetings is as yet safeguarded. Be that as it may, there is an expanding propensity for these midweek gatherings to become events for preaching or promotion, with the end goal of prayer packed away in the background.

Maybe, there are issues in a portion of our churches' midweek services which legitimize experimentation so as to look after attendances; however it is most likely critical that we monitor in the projects of our church periods explicitly set aside for supplication.

The church has a duty to keep alive the "spirit of prayer" among its members. If it disregards supplication, it is just normal for church members, generally, to follow that model in their own lives by giving less and less time to private petition. I accept the good old family special altar (old fashioned home altar) is a relic of times gone by in such a large number of Christian homes.

The testimony and services of the churches as organized units in the Master's service, and the individual lives of the members from the churches, will end up being inadequate except if both the churches and their members recognize the significance of supplication and provide for it the need it merits.

Be that as it may, when we do come to major in prayer, the spirituality of the lives of church members will be deepened, those members will turn out to be imperatively concerned in the salvation of the lost at home and around the globe (Evangelism), and they will begin to honor God with their means in an extent that will be acceptable to him, hence bringing into the Lord's treasury all the resources that are needed to extend every phase of his kingdom to the ends of the earth.

We Stand In Need Of Prayer

THE AVERAGE CHRISTIAN DOESN'T pray more because he (or she) has not had an extremely clear sentiment of his need of prayer. This makes it important that we all make another study of our need of fellowship with the Father in the light of his Word.

Prayer Cleanses The Heart From Sin

IN ANY CASE, WE ought to supplicate more for the purging (cleansing) of our individual hearts from sin. Alongside the psalmist, we should meditate upon our ways:

Who can discern his errors?

Clear thou me from hidden faults (Psalm 19:12 RSV).

Have mercy upon me, O God, according to thy lovingkindness:

According to the multitude of thy tender mercies blot out my transgressions.

Wash me thoroughly from mine iniquity,

And cleanse me from my sin…

Create in me a clean heart, O God;

And renew a right spirit within me (Psalm 51:1, 2, 10 KJV).

Prayer Gives Strength For Daily Tasks

IN ANY CASE, WE have to pray not the only one for individual cleansing from but, yet additionally that we may get the grace and strength for playing out the undertakings God would have us do. It is an exceedingly simple issue for the average Christian, not completely taught in God's Word, to neglect the way that he is entirely deficient in himself for carrying on with the acceptable life. Increasingly more every one of us needs to understand the profound noteworthiness of our Savior's declaration:

"I am the vine, ye are the branches: He that abideth in me, and I in him, the same beareth much fruit: for apart from me ye can do nothing" (John 15:5 KJV).

Prayer is the service line through which Jesus Christ's power flows into our hearts.

Besides, every Christian needs a new realization of the fact that all the power of Christ lies at the disposal of that believer who trusts in him completely and abides completely in him.

On this point we have not just the confirmation of Paul, who followed Christ all the more completely and making the most of his power more completely maybe than some other Christian who at any point lived, but in addition the reserved declaration of the Lord himself.

Paul's testimony was, "My God shall supply every need of yours according to his riches in glory in Christ Jesus" (Phil.4:19 KJV), while the qualified statement of Christ reads, "If ye abide in me, and my words abide in you, ask whatsoever ye will, and it shall be done unto you" (John 15:7 KJV).

What a world of encouragement is afforded every child of God in these outstanding passages, especially in the emphatic expressions of them! In Paul's statement the emphasis is upon "every." This implies there is positively no need of our own which our Lord will not supply, if we are in the right relation to him and approach him in prayer as we ought.

We need to make a distinction, in any case, between "our needs" and "our wants." The average individual "wants" a large number of things which he does not need-some of which would really demonstrate a disadvantage in the event that he had them.

That reality clarifies why God doesn't give us a great many of the things for which we ask. God answers each true prayer of his children, but he answers a significant number of them by declining to give us the things for which we ask, and filling in for those things which he denies us despite everything better things that we need.

In the consoling words from Jesus Christ the emphasis is on four points, two of them being conditions to acceptable prayer. The first of these is exemplified in the expression, "If ye abide in me," and the second, "and my words abide in you." Before we can claim Christ's great promise here, then, we must initially be in full fellowship with him and must be doing his revealed will.

If we meet these two major conditions we are prepared to claim the conceivable outcomes inferred in the rest of the entry, Ye shall "ask whatsoever ye will, and it shall be done unto you." Note the boundless prospects in the two watchwords here: "whatsoever," a word to which there is no restriction, and "will," which is as positive as language can communicate.

There can be positively no power in the Christian's life beside prayer, but all power is accessible to the Christian through acceptable prayer.

God Calls To Prayer

The Call Is Sounded
Throughout The Bible

IN ADDITION TO THE fact that God made it possible for his children to have power through prayer, but he earnestly desired that they should avail themselves of this power from day to day. More than that, he provided repeated commands to Christians to request that power.

So extraordinary is the goodness and generosity of the Heavenly Father that he gives us unqualified assurance of his desire to endue us with this power. Would we be able to envision any more noteworthy dignity for people than that they should experience and demonstrate the power of the God who made the universe? However this is his repeated promise as witness these passages chosen from among a large number of others of similar import:

Call unto me, and I will answer thee, and will show thee great things, and difficult, which thou knowest not (Jeremiah 33:3 KJV).

If my people, who are called by my name, shall humble themselves, and pray, and seek my face, and turn from their wicked ways; then will I hear from heaven, and will forgive their sin, and will heal their land (II Chronicles 7:14 ASV).

And it shall come to pass that before they call, I will answer; and while they are yet speaking, I will hear (Isaiah 45:11).

But thou, when thou prayest, enter into thine inner chamber, and having shut thy door, pray in thy Father who is in secret, and thy Father who seeth in secret shall recompense thee (Matthew 6:6 KJV).

God Stands Ready To Answer All Sincere Prayer

As per these promises God stands prepared to perform miracles in answer to genuine, sincere, acceptable prayer. He will forgive us our individual and social sins, evacuate the disciplines he has imposed upon us due to our defiance (disobedience), and expel the condemnations from our land. So anxious is God to bless us if we come into the right attitude he will even answer our prayers before we have had an opportunity to utter them.

So boundless, so unlimited is the Father's love for us that he even grants us the benefit of commanding him concerning work by his own hands. However, for our prayer life to be acceptable in his sight we should supplement our public prayers with our secret devotions, when none but God sees our mentalities (attitudes) and no ears but his hear the sincere articulation of our inner most thoughts.

In the light of all these wonderful revelations concerning God's command and promises concerning prayer, how might we account for the spiritual poverty of the average Christian? Have we not permitted Satan to swindle us of our greatest privilege?

Before we can claim God's promises in prayer, in any case, we must meet his conditions and pray in earnest.

The List Of Prayer Objects
Is Almost Unlimited

THERE ARE MANY CHRISTIANS who say they don't pray on the grounds that they don't have the foggiest idea what to pray to God for. Here again the Bible provides some timely help of every sincere seeker after truth by calling attention to them various things it is appropriate to look for in prayer. Just a few of these objects are recorded here.

A. Forgiveness of sins. "And forgive us our sins" (Luke 11:4 KJV).

B. Personal cleansing. "Create in me a clean heart, O God; And renew a right spirit within me" (Psalm 51:10 KJV).

C. Victory over temptation. "Watch and pray, that ye enter not unto temptation" (Matthew 26:41 KJV).

D. Our physical needs. "Give us this day our daily bread" (Matthew 6:11 KJV).

E. Our enemies. "Love your enemies, and pray for them that persecute you" (Matthew 5:44 NLT).

F. All men. "I exhort therefore, first of all, that supplications, prayers, intercessions, thanksgivings, be made for all men; for kings and all that are in high

place; that we may lead a tranquil and quiet life in all godliness and gravity"
(I Timothy 2:1, 2 ASV).

G. Recovery from sickness. "Is any among you sick? Let him call for thy elders of the church; and let them pray over him, anointing him with oil in the name of the Lord: and the prayer of faith shall save him that is sick, and the Lord shall raise him up; and if he have committed sins, it shall be forgiven him"
(James 5:14, 15).

H. Wisdom in solving problems. "But if any of you lacketh wisdom, let him ask of God, who giveth to all liberally and upbraideth not; and it shall be given him"
(James 1:5 ASV).

I. The Coming of Christ's Kingdom. "Thy kingdom come. Thy will be done, as in heaven so on earth"
(Matthew 6:10 KJV).

J. Additional laborers in God's vineyard. "Pray ye therefore the Lord of the harvest, that he send forth laborers into the harvest"
(Matthew 9:38 ASV).

K. One another. "Pray one for another"
(James 5:16 NKJV).

L. Our Missionaries. "Brethren, pray for us"
(I Thessalonians 5:25 NKJV).

In light of things for which we are justified in praying, it is needful that we recall the character of God, that he is our Heavenly Father, who is unquestionably more concerned for us than our own parents ever were, who has all our eventual benefits on a basic level, who is liberally, abundantly ready to supply all our genuine needs; and, as Jesus Christ reminded us in his teachings, our Father is far wiser in providing us good gifts than any earthly parent could possibly be.

There Are Many Hindrances To Prayer

1. Iniquity in the Heart. "If I regard iniquity in my heart, The Lord will not hear"
(Psalm 66:18 NKJV).

2. Unbelief. "But let him ask in faith, nothing doubting: for he that doubteth is like the surge of the sea driven by the wind and tossed. For let not that man think that he shall receive any thing of the Lord; a double-minded man, unstable in all his ways"
(James 1:6-8 ASV).

3. Selfishness. "Ye ask, and receive not, because ye ask amiss, that ye may spend it in your pleasures"
(James 4:3 ASV).

4. Pride. "God resisteth the proud, but giveth grace to the humble"
(James 4:6 ASV).

5. Unforgiving Spirit. "But if ye forgive not men their trespasses, neither will your Father forgive your trespasses"

(Matthew 6:15 ASV).

6. Neglect Of God's Word. "He that turneth away his ear from hearing the law, Even his prayer is an abomination"
    (Proverbs 28:9 ASV).

7. Disobedience. "Beloved, if our heart condemn us not, we have boldness toward God; and whatsoever we ask we receive of him, because we keep his commandments and do the things that are pleasing in his sight"
    (I John 3:21, 22 ASV).

For our encouragement let it be emphasized that when any of us is profoundly earnest about the matter of praying, God will provide to his with some timely help and help expel from his heart each deterrent that holds up traffic of worthy fellowship (acceptable communion) with his Father.

Prevailing Prayer Has "Four" Elements: (Adoration, Thanksgiving, Intercession and Petition)

1. Adoration in prayer comprises of the immediate love of God, as spoke to in the prologue to the Lord's Prayer, "Our Father who art in heaven, Hallowed be thy name." as such, reverence is revealing to God how we love and appreciate him and how much we desire to exalt his name.

2. Thanksgiving. Intently much the same as adoration, and oftentimes showed in both the Old Testament and

the New Testament as a fundamental component in prayer, however not explicitly referenced in the Lord's Prayer, is thanksgiving. Similarly as the earthly parent is delighted at the appreciation of his child, our Heavenly Father is pleased when we show genuine appreciation for those gifts, or blessings he has already offered to us.

3. Intercession. Intercession pleading with God on behalf of others, for example, requesting that he restore the sick to well-being, comfort the sorrowing, provide for the penniless (the needy), and bless the varied interests of his kingdom on the earth. This part of prayer was stressed by the Savior in the passage, "Thy kingdom come, Thy will be done, as in heaven, so on earth."

4. Petition. Then in prayer for forgiveness of sin, for delivery from temptation, and for daily bread we have representations of personal petitions. The Heavenly Father is interested in having us come before him with all our own personal needs, but for us to concentrate all our praying upon that part of petition is to neglect those bigger aspects of genuine prayer-love of the Father, Christ, and the Holy Spirit; earnest appreciation for God's past blessings; and intercession in behalf of the numerous phases of God's work in the earth and all of those in the world for whom we should count it a privilege to pray.

It is to a great extent as we practice ourselves in adoration, thanksgiving, and intercession that we truly grow in spiritual strength through prayer. Those who concentrate their efforts in prayer to approaching things exclusively for themselves will never become great Christians, on the grounds that until one's vision is stretched out to incorporate the whole world, and until he has built up a sense of genuine gratitude, his soul will continue dwarfed indeed.

Genuine Praying Is Hard Work

ONE OF THE PRINCIPLE reasons scarcely any Christians have grown great in prayer is that praying is hard work. It involves a psychological sharpness, focus, purpose, and earnestness of desire that are totally unfamiliar to the lazy soul. It is extremely simple consequently, as has just been hinted, for Satan to slip into our hearts and occupy us from our main purpose in prayer.

At the point when God's people in huge numbers start to pray truly, independently or in gatherings, at that point the insidious (evil one, the devil, Satan) one gets excited, for he realizes that God works through praying people. When God can work through his children, at that point, the power of darkness is bound to vanquish, doomed to defeat.

All Things Are Possible In Prayer

WHILE MUCH HAS JUST been suggested of the potential outcomes of prayer, there is need of further emphasis upon this extremely essential part of communion with God.

A portion of the additional passages recommending the enormous possibilities that lie open to all of us in prayer, if we are willing to pay God's price for power, follow:

"All things are possible to him that believeth"
(Mark 9:23 KJV)

"If ye have faith as a grain of mustard seed, ye shall say unto this mountain, Remove hence to yonder place; and it shall remove; and nothing shall be impossible unto you"
(Matthew 17:20 KJV).

"He that believeth on me, the works that I do shall he do also; and greater works than these shall he do; because I go unto the Father. And whatsoever ye shall ask in my name, that will I do, that the Father may be glorified in the Son. If ye shall ask anything in my name, that will I do."
(John 14:12-14 KJV).

"Ask, and it shall be given you; seek, and ye shall find; knock, and it shall be opened unto you: for every one that asketh receiveth; and he that seeketh findeth; and to him that knocketh it shall be opened."
(Matthew 7:7, 8 KJV).

Be that as it may, the full prospects of prayer have not been explored until we have appreciated one of the most heavenly, wondrous verses in the whole Bible: "Now unto him that is able to do exceedingly abundantly above all that we ask or think, according to the power that worketh in us"(Ephesians 3:20 KJV).

This verses discloses to us that so boundless is this power of God, thus liberal is his disposition toward us, his children, that he can do definitely more for us than we can ask, or even think.

At last, we read that when our Lord was upon the earth he every now and again spent entire nights in prayer. In the event that our Lord, who was very God as well as very man (100% God and 100% Man= THE GODMAN), required this fellowship with heaven so as to achieve his work completely and fully, how much more do we need to talk with God and seek his strength for the undertakings (tasks) that anticipate us?

Things To Do!
(For further study and research)

1. Few projects of Bible study could demonstrate all the more fascinating and beneficial than a careful searching of the Scriptures for everything said on prayer. A good concordance and parallel reference Bible will be of significant help.

2. You may line this up with a devotional reading of the great prayers of the Bible.

3. Make a study of God's promises to hear and answer prayer, as contained in both the Old and New Testaments.

4. Reread the Four Gospels and make a special memorandum on the prayer life of Jesus.

5. Select about six of the most outstanding promises of God to hear and answer prayer and put God to the test on them.

6. Attempt a half hour of Bible study and prayer every day at a good time for you in your day.

7. Start family prayer in your home.

8. Organize a Bible study/Prayer meeting in your home.

Chapter

TWO

Evangelism (Soul-Winners)

The Most Important Work In The World

Why Are We Not Soul-Winners?

WHAT NUMBER OF CHRISTIANS truly put forth any genuine attempt or invest in winning souls to Christ?

Since there are in a portion of our churches a few laborers who win many others to Christ as the years progressed, and a considerable lot of the callings are because of the works of pastors, preachers, and evangelists, the genuine number of soul-winners is far less than is expected.

Each Christian who has occupied themselves with winning souls will testify that winning souls for Christ brings larger fulfillments to the worker than some other phase of service on earth. The Bible additionally uncovers that the awards for soul-winning in the world to come will be larger than those for some other period of Christian effort wherein we can engage.

Why, at that point, do scarcely (so few) any Christians, nearly, participate in this highest of all forms of Christian service? The entire answer would include various variables, obviously, however a couple of the reasons which lie on a superficial level are introduced briefly:

Too Little Emphasis Given To Soul-Winning

VERY LITTLE EMPHASIS UPON this period of Christian service has been given in the churches, with the outcome that not many Christians feel any unmistakable duty (definite responsibility) regarding the salvation of the "lost."

Average Church Member Unprepared For The Task

THE AVERAGE CHURCH MEMBER, when he does consider the matter, feels entirely caught off guard for the errand (task) of soul-winning. He doesn't have a clue how to reach nor how to continue after the meeting with the prospect (the lost) has been acquired.

Our Example Nullifies Our Influence

IT IS THE BASIC excuse of many who are welcome to take part in close to home evangelism that their own lives present such a poor act of Christianity that they are embarrassed to request that an unsaved individual offer himself to the Savior.

We Have Little Compassion
For The Lost

Too few church members, evidently, have any compassion for the lost.

In any case, regardless of what our record in soul-winning in the past has been, or what the reasons of inert church individuals might be, the truth remains that it is workable for us to improve our Christian service along this line.

More than that, it is basic that we as people become soul-winners if we are to fulfill the needs and win the approval of him who redeemed us and who commissioned us to proceed with the activity of carrying his message of salvation to the lost until the last man, woman, boy, and girl on the earth have had a chance to be saved.

Also, as the Bible contains the main definitive word for Christians upon each other matter of obligation, so it is very full, clear, and decided on this generally significant of all phases of Christian service.

We Are Saved To Serve
Christ Called Us To Be Fishers Of Men

Indicating the primacy of soul-winning, Christ declared to his first disciples, Peter, Andrew, James, and John, the Galilean fishermen, when he initially called them, this would be their chief task. "Come ye after me, and I will make you fishers of men" (Matthew 4:19 ASV).

Back of the principle errand of the Christian, however, lies the essential assignment of the Savior himself when he came to earth, for as per Luke 19:10 ASV, "The Son of man came to seek and to save that which was lost."

Jesus Christ Expects Us To Carry The Gospel To The Whole World

IN ANY CASE, IT was not reliable with the great arrangement for Christ to stay upon the earth inconclusively after he had finished his ministry. Before he ascended to be everlastingly at the right hand of the Father, he entrusted the conveying of the message of salvation to the individuals who had just experienced the joy and the fulfillment of the regenerated life.

Somebody has determined that had the risen Savior, rather than returning to heaven, started a voyage through China or India, for instance, on the day that he rose, and had visited one town in that immense land every day, he would not yet have finished his appearance of that one nation, and the remainder of the world would yet be with no knowledge of him. Be that as it may, such a figuring expect a unimaginable speculation (an unthinkable hypothesis). Our Lord didn't attempt an unshared ministry to the world's billions. He enlisted men for the undertaking, promising his unfailing aid.

We Are Christ's Ambassadors To The Unsaved

FOR THOSE OF US who may hesitate to attempt to win others (lost souls) to Christ, it would help if we consider the confidence and trust the Lord has imposed in us by making us his representatives, not to a court in another land but to all the world. The average man would think of it as the most noteworthy respect of life in the event that he ought to be appointed by the President of the United States to turn into the American representative at any outside court, however in truth we have been charged as ambassadors of Jesus Christ, King of kings and Lord of lords! "We are ambassadors on behalf of Christ, as though God were entreating by us: we beseech you on behalf of Christ, be ye reconciled to God" (II Cor. 5:20 ASV).

Evangelism Is Our Major Task

The Salvation Of The Soul Is Fundamental

EVANGELISM IS THE SIGNIFICANT program of the church and the preeminent errand of the individual Christian. This is true for some reasons, however essentially in light of the fact that salvation is basic. There can be no spiritual growth in a person until he (or she) has first been born again and become a new creature in Jesus Christ.

We must major on Evangelism (leading lost souls to Christ). That is the main note in the marching orders of our risen Savior and Lord. Evangelism is the missionary spirit in action in real life.

It is the trailblazer and builder of churches. It is fundamental to all Christian expansion and must give its considerate influence to all sound teaching in the church.

"The church that ceases to be evangelistic will before long cease to be outreaching." It ceases to be evangelical. In the New Testament everything goes out from the churches and draws back into the churches. Whatever good might be done by methods and institutions apart from the churches, let us remember that Jesus Christ has placed his honor in the churches, and it should be urged with all emphasis that the hope of the people for a sound gospel, both for now and tomorrow, focuses in the churches of the living God.

"The church of the living God, the pillar and ground of truth." And the first and supreme business of every church is to win souls to the salvation and service of Jesus Christ. This work isn't optional, it is not secondary and incidental; it is primary and supreme. "As my Father hath sent me, even so send I you." The Son of man is come to seek and to save that which was lost" (AV).

If the seeking note for the salvation and training of souls be missing from a church, how much difference would there be between such a church and an ethical club? All the estates of a church are to go away from home, and stay abroad, in this Christly work of winning souls to Jesus Christ.

Churches Should Organize
For Soul-Winning

CHURCHES MUST RECOGNIZE EVANGELISM as their major task, but should compose and bless their labor with that in mind: Our supreme test is massing, assembling, and using our millions maybe billions of men and money, millions of missionary-minded men, women and youth under the direction of the Holy Spirit for the winning of the lost.

Soul-Winning Is An
Individual Responsibility

ONE OF THE GREATEST tragedies of all time is that the average Christian has permitted Satan to swindle him out of the joy of individual soul-winning. He crushes the Christian and makes him embarrassed, even ashamed to converse with other people who are lost about getting saved, becoming Christian, and hoodwinks him into the belief that he is not responsible for the salvation of others.

All through the Bible there is underscored the way that we are saved to serve-to do whatever we can to win to Christ those immediately around us who are lost, and afterward by our prayers, blessings, and lives to help with carrying the gospel to all the nations of the earth.

Jesus Christ Expects Each One
Of Us To Win Others

NOTE THE EMPHASIS WHICH God's Word places upon individual obligation (personal responsibility, moral duty) in soul-winning, as spoke to in a couple of passages from both the Old And New Testaments:

"Indeed, even so let your light shine before men; that they may see your good works, and glorify your Father who is in heaven" (Matthew 5:16 ASV) is an exhortation from Jesus Christ himself. Note that the emphasis in this passage is on "your," which is as individual or personal as it is conceivable to make it.

This implies every last one of us who has been saved man, woman, boy, or girl is compelled (under orders) from Christ

The Redeemer to do individual soul-winning. Not by any means the least of us is excused from that commitment.

We Will Be Held Accountable
For Our Failure To Do So

IN ADDITION TO THE fact that we are under commitment actually to win the lost to Christ, yet we will be considered responsible, accountable to God for our inability to do as such. Note the positiveness and directness of the Bible message upon this point.

Son of man, I have made thee a watchman unto the house of Israel; therefore hear the word at my mouth, and give them warning from me. When I say unto the wicked, Thou shalt surely die; and thou givest him not warning, nor speakest to warn the wicked from his wicked way, to save his life; the same wicked man shall die in his iniquity; but his blood will I require at thy hand. Yet if thou warn the wicked, and he turn not from his wickedness, nor from his wicked way, he shall die in his iniquity; but thou hast delivered thy soul (Ezekiel 3:17-19).

Considering this serious, God-imposed duty, how is the average Christian going to fare when he is censured on this issue at the judgment seat of Jesus Christ?

Our Responsibility Begins At Home

OUR RESPONSIBILITY AS INDIVIDUAL soul-winners begins in our own homes and reaches out to the ends of the earth. We remember the story of the vicious demoniac (demon possessed young man) of Gadara who was healed by the Savior and restored to his right mind, and who needed to show his appreciation (gratitude) for what the Lord Jesus Christ had done for him by accompanying him on his ministry.

There was little help he could perform by just joining the Lord's gathering, but there was an extraordinary plan he could filfull do by giving his own testimony to God's power among his own close family, relatives, and friends; so it was consummately common that Jesus Christ "sent him away saying, Return to thy house, and declare how great things God hath done for thee. What's more, he went his way, publishing all through the whole city how great things Jesus had done for him" (Luke 8:38, 39 ASV).

Furthermore, if this man out of whom Jesus Christ had quite recently cast out brutal evil (demons) presences could turn into a successful witness, by what means can we who have been equipped with normal faculties for our whole lives say that we can't testify for our Savior? Furthermore, note the simplicity of the message this recently redeemed man was to pass on to other people.

He basically revealed to them how great things Jesus Christ had done for him. Each Christian who wants to win souls could unquestionably repeat the "story of his own transformation (conversion)," which even the great missionary Paul did over and again in his testimonies for Christ.

It will likely help us with understanding our duty in the matter of winning souls in the event that we refresh our minds on God's interest for the unsaved, as set forth in this striking passage from the pen of Peter:

"The Lord is not slack concerning his promise, as some count slackness; but is longsuffering to you-ward, not wishing that any should perish, but that all should come to repentance" (II Peter 3:9 ASV).

Since God wills that none should perish, and has chosen us as the flag-bearers (the messengers) to convey the knowledge on salvation to all men all over the earth, most likely he is looking to every one of us who has accepted to help convey the gospel offer to every single unsaved man far and wide.

All around every last one of us there are truly a large number of lost people, a significant number of whom without a doubt are looking to us to present to them the message of redemption. Would you be able to envision their mistake when they understand that we don't think enough about our Christianity to attempt to carry others to grasp it? Consider the possibility that these unsaved ones ought to go into forever lost, and should meet us with censuring eyes at God's judgment bar and ask, "Gracious, for what reason didn't you caution us of our approaching fate.

A large number of lost souls on this day of final reckoning and most likely all through all time everlasting will be howling to themselves, "No man careth for my soul" (Psalm 142:4 ASV)!

Today's Opportunities May Be Gone Tomorrow

BEFORE WE CAN START to match our obligations as close to home soul-winners we should understand that the chances of today might be gone tomorrow, and every now and again these open doors will stay away forever.

Else we may defer our purpose to speak to the unsaved about us until these people are gone, and we will need to answer to our Lord, as did one of old, "And as thy servant was busy here and there, he was gone" (I Kings 20:40 ASV).

Everyone Can Win Souls

The Holy Spirit Will Supply Worker's Needs

IT IS RECOGNIZED, OBVIOUSLY, that the average Christian declares that he is absolutely unequipped for winning lost souls to Christ. However, has that one at any point put forth a true attempt toward that path to see whether he could succeed or not? Does he not comprehend that the Holy Spirit stands prepared to go with him as he goes forward on an evangelistic mission, and supply all his needs?

Boys And Girls Should Be Won To Jesus Christ Early In Life

EVERY SOUL-WINNER SHOULD REMEMBER that it is far simpler to win young men and young ladies to the Savior than it is to win grown-up people. This doesn't imply that we ought to disregard people in our evangelistic endeavors, but that, in light of a legitimate concern for accomplishing bigger outcomes, just as in the expectation of winning the whole life just as the soul of the individual, we ought to be tenacious in our endeavors to win the young men and young ladies. Figures have been assembled such that nine people out of ten who become Christians do as such before they are seventeen years of age.

This implies except if we win young men and young ladies to Christ before they arrive at that age the odds are nine to one they will go through life and into eternity without Christ.

Our Field Is The World – A Worldwide Commission

OUR WHOLE OBLIGATION IN carrying Christ's commission to make him known to the unsaved has not been done when we have merely addressed the lost promptly about us and looked to carry them to an acceptance of Jesus Christ. That is simply the beginning stage in our evangelistic undertaking. Our full assignment has not been practiced until we have done everything within our power in proclaiming Christ's power to save to the last lost individual in the whole world.

Christ stated, "The field is the world" (Matthew 13:38 KJV). Not only is our field the world, however we have distinct orders from the Savior to take his gospel to all nations: "Go ye therefore, and make disciples of the nations" (Matthew 28:19 KJV). This worldwide order of Christ is emphasized further in these words:

"Go ye into all the world, and preach the gospel to the whole creation" (Mark 16:15 KJV).

"And that repentance and remission of sins should be preached in his name unto all the nations, beginning from Jerusalem" (Luke 24:47 ASV).

"And ye shall be my witnesses both in Jerusalem, and in all Judea and Samaria, and unto the uttermost part of the earth" (Acts 1:8 KJV).

"We must work the works of him that sent me, while it is day: the night cometh, when no man can work" (John 9:4 ASV). If each of us would heed this warning from the Master himself we would make opportunity now to redeem our failures of the past.

The Soul-Winner Needs Equipment

To do successful (effective) soul-winning a Christian must have among others, the accompanying personal capabilities, as indicated by God's Word:

1. Compassion for the lost-Psalm 126:5,6; Romans 10:1.

2. Personal Purity-Psalm 51:10-13; 66:18.

3. Knowledge of The Bible-Ephesians 6:17.

4. Wisdom-Proverbs 11:30.

5. Faith – Mark 9:23; Isaiah 55:11.

6. Patience – Ecclesiastes 11:1.

7. Tact – Matthew 10:16.

8. Diligence – Acts 20:31.

9. Spiritual Power – Acts 1:8.

The Soul-Winner Gains Rich Satisfactions

There is a more splendid side to this question of the stewardship of evangelism, and that involves the satisfactions which the soul-winner reaps in this life, and the inexhaustible rewards which God lays up for him in the world to come.

One of the satisfactions that go to the soul-winner, and likely the least one of all, is that of a reasonable inner voice (a clear conscience): "Yet if thou warn the wicked, and he turn not from his wickedness, nor from his wicked way, he shall die in his iniquity; but thou hast delivered thy soul" (Ezekiel 3:19 ASV).

Unquestionably more satisfying than the negligible satisfaction of a clear conscience is the realization of the benefit one has presented upon others in bringing them into a knowledge of salvation: "Let him know, that he who converteth a sinnere from the error of his way shall save a soul from death, and shall cover a multitude of sins" (James 5:20).

Intently much the same as the joy of saving souls from death is the realization of the fact that the soul-winner's influence upon others is for the most part inspiring, uplifting: "How beautiful upon the mountains are the feet of him that bringeth good tidings of good, that publisheth salvation, that saith unto Zion, Thy God reigneth!" (Isaiah 52:7).

Moreover, the soul-winner "gathereth fruit unto life eternal" (John 4:36). He will be proud to present to the Master proof of his labors; for

"He that goeth forth and weepeth, bearing seed for sowing,

"Shall doubtless come again with joy, bringing his sheaves with him" (Psalm 126:6).

That those who have been faithful in soul-winning on earth will shine in the brilliance of God's glory forever in the world to come, we are assured in this passage: "And they that are wise shall shine as the brightness of the firmament; and they that turn many to righteousness as the stars for ever and ever" (Daniel 12:3).

This is the most distinct assurance of outstanding recognition in heaven that is given in the whole Bible. It would be completely conflicting with the spirit of genuine Christianity for us to need to stand out in heaven, for we should endeavor to win many souls all together that we may honor our Redeemer, Jesus Christ who bought our salvation by his dying on the cross.

Yet, it is fascinating to realize that those of us who honor Christ in our lives will be greatly honored by the Father in the life to come.

At the point when this life is ended, and we go out to be with God, we will find that we are rewarded for each spirit we have won to Christ the Savior by our own personal effort, our public testimony, our consistent Christian conduct, our teaching and our proclaiming, and our blessings to missions which bring about sending the gospel to the unsaved beyond our communities, in our states, in the nation at large, and around the globe.

Furthermore, the more souls we win in this life the fuller and richer will our existence in heaven be all through the long, long eternity.

For Further Study and Research

1. Read and Study The Believer's Guide On Personal Evangelism – by Reverend Dr.
    John Thomas Wylie.

2. Familiarize yourself with the fundamental Scripture passages on the plan of salvation, embodying such topics as:

    a. "All have sinned" (Romans 3:10-12, 23 ASV)

b. "The Wages of sin is death" (Romans 6:23; Ezekiel 3:18 ASV)

c. "All must be born again: (John 3:1-16 ASV)

d. "We are saved by grace, through faith, and not by works" (Ephesians 2:8, 9 ASV)

e. "Youth is the best time to be saved" (Ecclesiastes 12:1 ASV)

f. "Christ will not turn away any sinner who comes to him" (John 6:37 ASV)

g. "Behold, now is the acceptable time" (II Corinthians 6:2 KJV)

h. "Thou shalt find him, when thou searchest after him with all thy heart and with all thy soul" (Deuteronomy 4:29 KJV)

Chapter

THREE

The Master's "Well-Done!"

THE BIBLE GIVES US motivation to accept that there will be degrees of rewards in heaven relying on our faithfulness in this life. We can't conjecture on the character of these rewards, however we can accept that God has uncovered this fact as an upgrade to faithfulness and effort.

It is unimaginable to expect to guess that the church member who disregards his spiritual duties will have a similar status in heaven as the good steward who gives himself and his means unsparingly for the cause of Jesus Christ. For the last mentioned, heaven will begin with his Master's approving "Well Done!"

Be that as it may, the reward of the faithful isn't totally conceded to what's to come. Loyalty to Jesus Christ and his church brings present felicities just as well as lasting joys to come. The genuinely cheerful (happy) Christian is the committed Christian, whose satisfaction is in the joy of service, and for whom heaven has begun below. What are some of the rewards of faithful stewardship?

The Faithful Steward Has A Good Conscience

ONE EXPLANATION SCARCELY SO few Christians are really happy is that their consciences hurt them, not generally in light of the fact that they have committed some shocking, immoral act, but because they have neglected to live up to the exclusive standards of stewardship which they realize God has set for them.

Be that as it may, the Christian who sets aside out of his pay, before he spends any of it on himself, and satisfactory portion for God's cause, who uses his time, gifts, influence, and all his other assets for the glory of God, is truly happy, because his conscience is unmistakably clear and he enjoys in his mind and heart the approval of the Lord.

Paul, who carried on with the most difficult Christian life of all followers of Jesus Christ through all the ages, gave himself and every one of his powers all the more energetically to the service of the Master, following his conversion, than some other has done. It is no big surprise, that Paul was able to declare, "Brethren, I have lived before God in all good conscience until this day" (Acts 23:1 KJV).

The upkeep of this attitude was an unmistakable approach (a definite policy) with this apostle, for he sought to keep his conscience intelligible (clear) toward his kindred men, just as toward God, as set out in his words, "Herein I also exercise a conscience void of offence toward God and men always" (Acts 24:16 ASV).

When the mother of James and John, without further ado before Christ's torturous killing (the crucifixion), went to the Savior and asked that her sons may sit, one on the right hand and the other on the left of the Lord in his kingdom, Jesus answered that these places of great honor were reserved by the Father, to be filled as he had planned.

We may believe that eternity will have its astonishments in the bestowment of divine honor. Some who expected preferment will be baffled. Other people who gave no thought to personal increase will be commended and exalted. Who can question (doubt) that Paul will be conspicuous among the last mentioned?

It isn't allowed to any of us to coordinate the gifts and services of Paul, obviously, however in the event that every last one of us should match our abilities and opportunities with even a small segment of the business and steadfastness that described the great Apostle to the Gentiles, we would insure ourselves a very happy sojourn here on earth and a rich compensation (an abundant reward) in heaven. God rewards as per abilities and faithfulness, we will remember, "And to whomsoever much is given, of him will much be required: and to whom they commit much, of him will they ask the more" (Luke 12:48 ASV).

While the satisfaction of a good conscience is an enormous motivating, great incentive to faithful stewardship, a much higher thought is the approval of God, of which the faithful steward is constantly assured. From a copious volume of teaching in the Bible we are persuaded that God never permits the smallest service to him or needy humankind, in his name to go unrewarded.

We quote just a couple of passages to suggest the approval of the Lord's faithful stewards, especially in the matter of putting the claims of God first, honoring him with our means, and winning the lost to our Saviour Jesus Christ.

"Honor Jehovah with thy substance,
And with the first-fruits of all thine increase:
So shall thy barns be filled with plenty,
And thy vats shall overflow with new wine"
(Proverbs 3:9, 10 ASV).

"The liberal soul shall be made fat;
And he that watereth shall be watered also himself"
(Proverbs 11:25 ASV).

"Wheresoever the gospel shall be preached throughout the whole world, that also which this woman hath done shall be spoken of for a memorial of her"

(Mark 14:9 ASV).

"Give, and it shall be given unto you; good measure, pressed down, shaken together, running over, shall they give into your bosom. For with what treasure ye mete it shall be measured to you again" (Luke 6:38 ASV).

"He that soweth sparingly shall reap also sparingly; and he that soweth bountifully shall reap also bountifully" (II Corinthians 9:6 ASV).

We Share In Extending God's Kingdom

ANOTHER EXTRAORDINARY SATISFACTION OF the faithful steward is what originates from the knowledge that he has an unequivocal offer in expanding God's kingdom in the world. Again and again in the Bible we are assured that the Lord never permits one of his servants to go unrewarded for any deed of service, regardless of how humble that service might be.

Indeed, even one kind word addressed to an unsaved soul or discouraged person, or one cup of cold water given to a parched (thirsty) person for the sake of the Savior Jesus Christ is always recognized and rewarded by the kind Heavenly Father.

For our support how about we look at a couple of direct passages from our infallible guide, the Word of God:

"Cast thy bread upon the waters; for thou shalt find it after many days."
(Ecclesiastes 11:1 ASV).

"Blessed are ye that sow beside all waters."
(Isaiah 32:20 ASV).

"He that goeth forth and weepoeth, bearing seed for sowing, Shall doubtless come again with joy, bring his sheaves with him."
(Psalm 126:6 ASV).

"How beautiful upon the mountains are the feet of him that bringeth good tidings, that publisheth peace, that bringeth good tidings of good, that publisheth salvation, that saith unto Zion, Thy God reigneth!"
(Isaiah 52:7 ASV).

There is no doubt that each person who is faithful in the exercise of his stewardship, not alone of means but of time, talents, influence, prayer, soul-winning, and the various resources at the Christian's command, will have a definite share in extending God's kingdom in the world and will begin to reap dividends upon those investments even in this world.

Bible students will remember the account of David's division of spoils, following his fruitful assault (successful raid) upon the Amalekites, when the future king of Israel recovered not just his two spouses who had been taken from him, but a large amount of spoils of varied character as well.

David had left some of his weaker men at the camp, while he and his capable followers made the raid that brought about the capture and slaughter of the adversary (enemy). A portion of those who went into battle restricted any division of the spoils with those who guarded the baggage at the camp, yet David showed his wisdom and humanity by ordering:

"For as his share is that goeth down to the battle, so shall his share be that tarrieth by the baggage: they shall share alike" (I Samuel 30:24 ASV).

This same principle is placed into activity in his kingdom by the all-wise, just, and honest Heavenly Father. He assures the faithful men and women, who invest their prayers, endowments (gifts), and other assets in extending the kingdom, that they will share equally with the missionaries, evangelists, ministers, and other laborers who minister to needy humanity in the name of our Lord and Savior, Jesus Christ.

We all can have a clear and liberal share in extending Christ's kingdom all through the world if we would become faithful servants of God while we live.

At times the Lord may have an alternate plan by which we should practice our stewardship than that which we had preferred for ourselves; however we all will perceive that his plan is far superior than our own and should be followed no matter what, and at all costs.

Our Eternal Dividends Are In The Bank Of Heaven

NOT ONLY DOES THE faithful servant (or loyal steward) of the considerable number of assets which God has given him enjoy a good conscience, a sense of God's endorsement (approval) here on earth, and a share in extending Christ's kingdom out to the ends of the earth, but also he lays up for himself eternal dividends in the bank of heaven whereupon he may draw similarly as vigorously as he prefers each day throughout the endless eternity.

It was in the hope of enabling all of his children to enjoy an inexhaustible passage into paradise and the largest satisfactions there that the Master admonished us in his earthly ministry upon this very point:

"Lay not up for yourselves treasures upon the earth, where moth and rust consume, and where thieves break through and steal: but lay up for yourselves treasures in heaven, where neither moth nor rust doth consume, and where thieves do not break through nor steal" (Matthew 6:19, 20 ASV).

Droughts, starvations (famines), wars, and different catastrophes can clear away even authentic life reserve funds without prior warning; those investments which we have made in heaven through commitments of our means and our service in the kingdom of God, can't be touched by the economic reverses here on earth.

Our investments in stewardship are deposited by our Lord for us in the Eternal Bank of Heaven. There is no power in all the universe that can deny us of them, nor can any evil power or force intrude on the steady progression of the liberal dividends God pays. If we have been faithful in our stewardship as servants of Christ, we may certainly expect that we will be very rich in the world to come.

The beloved Paul supplemented our Master's counsel on eternal investments with a sharp notice against covetousness:

"Charge them that are rich in this present world, that they be not highminded, nor have their hope set on the uncertainty of riches, but on God, who giveth us richly all things to enjoy; that they do good, that they be rich in good works, that they be ready to distribute, willing to communicate; laying up in store for themselves a good foundation against the time to come, that they may lay hold on the life which is life indeed." (I Timothy 6:17-19 ASV).

Self-centeredness, selfishness and covetousness are not constrained to the rich, it must be remembered. The poor man who won't honor God with what he has might be similarly as great a sinner according to God just like the rich man who will not give generously. God is more interested in thought processes (motives) and spirit than he is in the size of one's gift.

God Shall Commend Us
On The Last Day!

THE PROPORTION OF OUR fulfilment all through all eternity will be dictated by the reception which Christ welcomes us when we face him at his judgment seat on the last day.

The Lord reads all the plans and intents of our minds and hearts. No disguise, affectation, or bragging can pass the eye God undetected. If after Christ has read and approved our record on earth, he invites us to his eternal abode with, "Well Done, good and faithful servant: ... enter thou into the joy of thy Lord," our joy will be incomparable (supreme) every day of the vast eternity.

However, if we have simply trust Christ for salvation here on earth, and have done no service an in expression of our love and gratitude of everything he accomplished for us, what prospect of reward will be our own? Our souls will have been saved, but our lives will be empty of fruit. As the accompanying clarifies, faithfulness will be the basis of commendation:

"And he that received the five talents came and brought other five talents, saying, Lord, thou deliveredest unto me five talents: lo, I have gained other five talents. His lord said unto him, Well done, good and faithful servant: thou hast been faithful over a few things, I will set thee over many things" (Matthew 25:20, 21 ASV).

One of the empowering parts of this study is managed in the way that the Lord will reward us for many humble modest services we have unknowingly performed for him, as set out in this fascinating proclamation from Christ himself.

"But when the Son of man shall come in his glory, and all the angels with him, then shall he sit on the throne of his glory: and before him shall be gathered all the nations: and he shall separate them one from another, as the shepherd separateth the sheep from the goats; and he shall set the sheep on his right hand, but the goats on the left."

"Then shall the King say unto them on his right hand, Come, ye blessed of my Father, inherit the kingdom prepared for you from the foundation of the world: for I was hungry, and ye gave me to eat; I was thirsty, and ye gave me drink; I was a stranger, and ye took me in; naked, and ye clothed me; I was sick, and ye visited me; I was in prison, and ye came unto me."

"Then shall the righteous answer him, saying, Lord, when saw we thee hungry, and fed thee? Or athirst, and gave thee drink? And when saw we thee a stranger, and took thee in? Or naked, and clothed thee?"

"And when saw we thee sick, or in prison, and came unto thee? And the King shall answer and say unto them, Verily I say unto you, Inasmuch as ye did it unto one of these my brethren, even these least, ye did it unto me."

"Then shall he say also unto them on the left hand, Depart from me, ye cursed, into the eternal fire which is prepared for the devil and his angels: for I was hungry, and ye did not give me to eat; I was thirsty, and ye gave me no drink; I was a stranger, and ye took me not in; naked, and ye clothed me not; sick, and in prison, and ye visited me not. Then shall they also answer, saying, Lord, when saw we hungry, or athirst, or a stranger, or naked, or sick, or in prison, and did not minister unto thee?"

"Then shall he answer them, saying, Verily I say unto you, Inasmuch as ye did it not unto one of these least, ye did it unto me. And these shall go away into eternal punishment: but the righteous into eternal life" (Matthew 25:31-46 ASV).

Be that as it may, it isn't vital that we hold up until we get to heaven to start reaping the fulfillments (satisfactions) and rewards from our wholehearted loyalty and faithfulness to Jesus Christ, a fact that is moreover clarified by a direct statement of the Lord himself:

"Jesus said, Verily I say unto you, There is no man that hath left house, or brethren, or sisters, or mother, or father, or children, or lands, for my sake, and for the gospel's sake, but he shall receive a hundredfold now in this time, houses, and brethren, and sisters, and mothers, and children, and lands, with persecutions; and in the world to come eternal life" (Mark 10:29, 30 ASV).

The commendation and reward for faithful service have already been given and been provided in heaven anticipating the arrival of the servant in the presence of his Lord, according to the inspired Paul, who wrote:

"I have fought the good fight, I have finished the course, I have kept the faith: henceforth there is laid up for me the crown of righteousness, which the Lord, the righteous judge, shall give to me as that day; and not to me only, but also to all them that have loved his appearing" (II Timothy 4:7, 8 ASV).

Except for his initial persecution of the church, in which he engaged with a clear conscience, Paul presumably had fewer things on his record to blushed for, when he was called into the presence of the Savior, than any other one who has ever lived.

Thus far as the record is accessible to us, no doubt he had larger rewards laid up for him in heaven than any others; for doubtlessly no other follower of whom we know at any point gave himself so wholeheartedly and faithfully to the service of Christ.

Not many endured more noteworthy hardships (greater hardships) than he, and practically independent, however he was sustained to a limited extent by some of the churches and a few helpers, he delivered the gospel to nearly the whole known world, and that in a day when the techniques for movement and correspondence were not a tenth so various, advantageous, and productive as they are today.

Imagine a scenario in which Christians of today, even you and I, could get Paul's spirit for this generation? We could convey the gospel in its transforming power to the rest of the world within our own lifetime.

Sin, with all its numerous chaperon shades of malice, could be greatly restrained in the world; and that wonderful day when "the earth will be filled with the knowledge of the glory of the Lord, as the waters cover the sea" (Hab. 2:14 RSV) could be hastened.

Bibliography

The Apostolic Preaching And Its Developments (1944), (new edition) London, Eng.: Hodder & Stoughton, LTD

Morton, E. S. (1929) The Place Of Morality In The Thought Of Paul. Chester, PA.: (Publisher UNK)

Primitive Christianity In Its Contemporary Setting (1956) New York, NY.: Living Age Books, Meridan Books

The Ethics Of Paul (1957) Nashville, TN.: Abingdon Press, Apex Books.

The Holy Bible (1964) Authorized King James Version. Chicago, Ill.: J. G. Ferguson

The Holy Bible (1982) New International Version. Grand Rapids, MI.: Thomas Nelson (Used By Permission)

The Holy Bible (1978) New York, NY.: New York International Bible Society (Used By Permission)

The Holy Bible (1953) The Revised Standard Version. Nashville, TN.: Thomas Nelson & Sons (Used By Permission)

The Holy Bible (1901) The American Standard Version. Nashville, TN.: Thomas Nelson (Used By Permission)

The Holy Bible (1959) The Berkeley Version. Grand Rapids, MI.: Zondervan (Used By Permission)

The Holy Bible (1977) The New American Standard Bible. USA.: The Lockman Foundation (Used By Permission)

The Holy Bible (1996) The New Living Translation. Wheaton, Ill.: Tyndale House Publishers (Used By Permission)

The New Testament In The Language Of The People (1937, 1949) Chicago, Ill.: Charles B. Williams, Bruce Humphries, Inc, The Moody Bible Institute (Used By Permission)

The New Testament In Modern English (1958) New York, NY.: J. B. Phillips, Macmillan (Used By Permission)

The Wycliff Bible Commentary (1962, 1968) Nashville, TN.: Chicago, Ill.:

The Southwestern Company, The Moody Bible Institute Of Chicago

About The Author

THE REVEREND DR. JOHN Thomas Wylie is one who has dedicated his life to the work of God's Service, the service of others; and being a powerful witness for the Gospel of Our Lord and Savior Jesus Christ. Dr. Wylie was called into the Gospel Ministry June 1979, whereby in that same year he entered The American Baptist College of the American Baptist Theological Seminary, Nashville, Tennessee.

As a young Seminarian, he read every book available to him that would help him better his understanding of God as well as God's plan of Salvation and the Christian Faith. He made a commitment as a promising student that he would inspire others as God inspires him. He understood early in his ministry that we live in times where people question not only who God is; but whether miracles are real, whether or not man can make a change, and who the enemy is or if the enemy truly exists.

Dr. Wylie carried out his commitment to God, which has been one of excellence which led to his earning his Bachelors of Arts in Bible/Theology/Pastoral Studies. Faithful and obedient to the call of God, he continued to matriculate in his studies earning his Masters of Ministry from Emmanuel Bible College, Nashville, Tennessee & Emmanuel Bible College, Rossville, Georgia. Still, inspired to please the Lord and do that which is well – pleasing in the Lord's sight, Dr. Wylie recently on March 2006, completed his Masters of Education degree with a concentration in Instructional Technology earned at The American Intercontinental University, Holloman Estates, Illinois. Dr. Wylie also previous to this, earned his Education

Specialist Degree from Jones International University, Centennial, Colorado and his Doctorate of Theology from The Holy Trinity College and Seminary, St. Petersburg, Florida.

Dr. Wylie has served in the capacity of pastor at two congregations in Middle Tennessee and Southern Tennessee, as well as served as an Evangelistic Preacher, Teacher, Chaplain, Christian Educator, and finally a published author, writer of many great inspirational Christian Publications such as his first publication:

"Only One God: Who Is He?" – published August 2002 via formally 1ˢᵗ books library (which is now AuthorHouse Book Publishers located in Bloomington, Indiana & Milton Keynes, United Kingdom) which caught the attention of **The Atlanta Journal Constitution Newspaper.**

Dr. Wylie is happily married to Angel G. Wylie, a retired Dekalb Elementary School teacher who loves to work with the very young children and who always encourages her husband to move forward in the Name of Jesus Christ. They have Four children, 11 grand-children and one great-grandson all of whom they are very proud. Both Dr. Wylie and Angela Wylie serve as members of the Salem Baptist Church, located in Lilburn, Georgia, where the Reverend Dr. Richard B. Haynes is Senior pastor.

Dr. Wylie has stated of his wife: "she knows the charm and beauty of sincerity, goodness, and purity through Jesus Christ. Yes, she is a Christian and realizes the true meaning of loveliness as the reflection as her life of holy living gives new meaning, hope, and purpose to that of her husband, her children, others may say of her, "Behold the handmaiden of the Lord." A Servant of Jesus Christ!

This publication, "The Master's Well-Done," is a book on The Stewardship of Prayer, Evangelism (Soul-winning), and The Master's Well-Done.

The First Phase of our publication is concerned about the Stewardship of Prayer. Many churches in the land, just as a considerable lot of its individuals from those churches, have neglected to profit themselves of the spiritual power that may be theirs if they followed the claim of early Christians and tarried in the upper room until they, as well, were endued with power from on high.

Many Christians experience life with their spirits incredibly undernourished spiritually, and that amidst God's boundless abundance from which we are allowed to choose those nourishments that are expected to make us strong, happy, and useful in the service of the Lord. "We have not because we ask not."

The second phase of this publication concerns Soul-Winning (Evangelism). What number of individuals from your church truly put forth any genuine attempt to win others (souls) to Christ?

Since there are in a portion of our churches a few laborers who win various others to Christ during the year, and a significant number of the callings are because of the works of ministers, evangelists, preachers, the genuine number of soul-winners is far less than what we would anticipate.

Each Christian who has ever occupied themselves with it will affirm that triumphant spirits carries larger fulfillments to the laborer than some other phase of service on earth. The Bible likewise reveals that the rewards for soul-winning on the earth to come will be bigger than those for some other phase of Christian effort in which we can engage.

At long last the third phase of this publication concerns the Master's Well-Done. The Bible gives us reason to believe that there will be degrees of reward in heaven depending on our faithfulness in this life. We can't theorize on the character of these rewards, however we can expect that God has revealed this truth as a stimulus to loyalty and effort. It is beyond imagination or not possible to suppose that the church member who neglects spiritual responsibilities will have the status in heaven as the good steward who gives himself and his means unsparingly for the cause of Jesus Christ. For the latter, heaven will begin with his Master's approving "Well-Done."

However, the reward of the faithful Christian is not all deferred to the future. Loyalty to Jesus Christ and his church brings present felicities as well as lasting joys to come. The truly happy Christian is the committed Christian whose happiness is in the joy of service, and for whom heaven awaits.